W9-DJA-597

WHAT IS A DATABASE?

Kirsty Holmes

COMPUTERS
AND
<CODING>

KidHaven
PUBLISHING

Published in 2019 by KidHaven Publishing, an Imprint of Greenhaven Publishing, LLC
353 3rd Avenue, Suite 255, New York, NY 10010

© 2019 Booklife Publishing

This edition is published by arrangement with Booklife Publishing.

Written by: Kirsty Holmes
Edited by: Holly Duhig
Designed by: Danielle Jones

Cataloging-in-Publication Data

Names: Holmes, Kirsty.
Title: What is a database? / Kirsty Holmes.
Description: New York : KidHaven Publishing, 2019. | Series: Computers and coding | Includes glossary and index.
Identifiers: ISBN 9781534527201 (pbk.) | ISBN 9781534527195 (library bound) | ISBN 9781534527218 (6 pack)
Subjects: LCSH: Databases--Juvenile literature. | Web databases--Juvenile literature.
Classification: LCC QA76.9.D32 H645 2019 | DDC 005.74--dc23

IMAGE CREDITS

Cover – izabel.l, 1000s_pixels, Macrovector, danjazzia. 4 – Sudowoodo. 6 – Petr Vaclavek, Sudowoodo. 7 – Sudowoodo. 8 – Antonio Francois.
10 – art.tkach. 11 – ideyweb. 14 – Dacian G. 16-17 – Sentavio. 18 – Sudowoodo. 19 – Kit8.net. 20 – Sudowoodo, Ji-eun Lee. 21 – Sudowoodo, TORWAISTUDIO. 22 –
Sudowoodo, Iconic Bestiary, Alina F. 23 – Sudowoodo.

Printed in the United States of America

CPSIA compliance information: Batch #BS18KL: For further information contact Greenhaven Publishing LLC, New York, New York at 1-844-317-7404.

WHAT IS A DATABASE?

COMPUTERS AND <CODING>

Words that look like **this** can be found in the glossary on page 24.

WHAT IS DATA?

Data is another word for information. Facts, figures, numbers, and lists are all types of data.

HOW MANY BOYS LIKE MUSIC?

HOW MANY LIKE ICE CREAM?

HOW MANY BIRTHDAYS IN JANUARY?

HOW MANY GIRLS PLAY SOCCER?

Data helps us understand the world around us.

Data collected about one specific **topic** is called a dataset. For example, your teacher will collect a dataset about all the people in your class.

NAME	AGE	ADDRESS	FAVORITE SUBJECT
John	8	1 Denney Road	Math
Kelby	7	31 Windsor Gardens	Music
Holly	8	221a Baker Street	Science
Alex	7	28 Acacia Road	Geography
Danielle	7	712 Maple Street	Art
Drue	8	3 Privet Drive	Computers
Garrett	8	1 Downs Street	Gym
Dan	7	123 Conch Street	English

WHAT IS A DATABASE?

Some datasets are small, but others can have thousands or even millions of separate pieces of information.

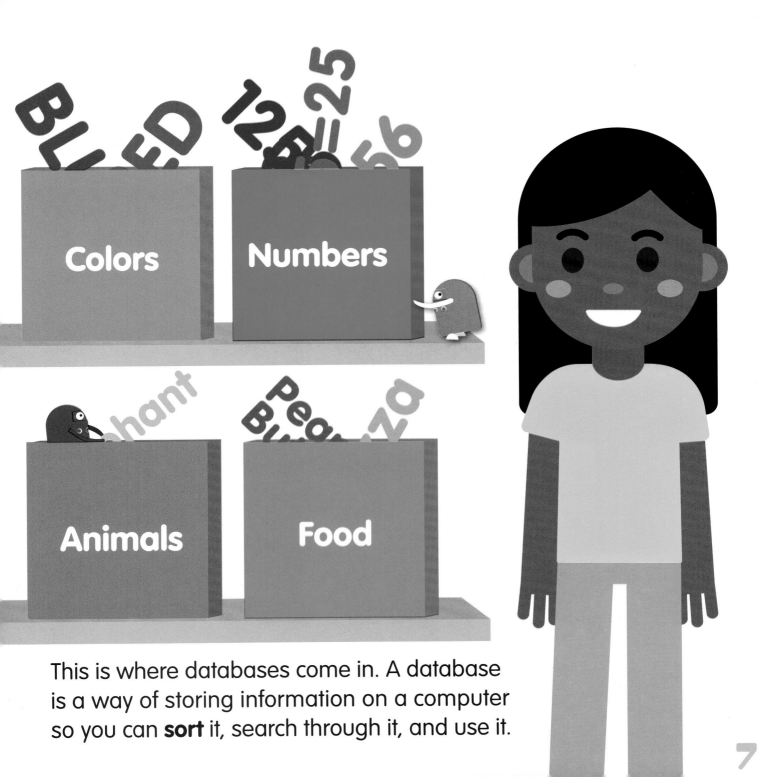

This is where databases come in. A database is a way of storing information on a computer so you can **sort** it, search through it, and use it.

SIMPLE DATABASES

A simple database is a computer program that a computer can use to store and **access** a dataset.

Address Book

John
1 Denney Road
555-8761

Alex
28 Acacia Road
758-8641

Danielle
712 Maple Street
687-4531

Garrett
1 Downs Street
547-2385

Some databases are used for small or simple datasets, like an address book. Each entry is called a record.

Databases sort information into columns, rows, and fields.

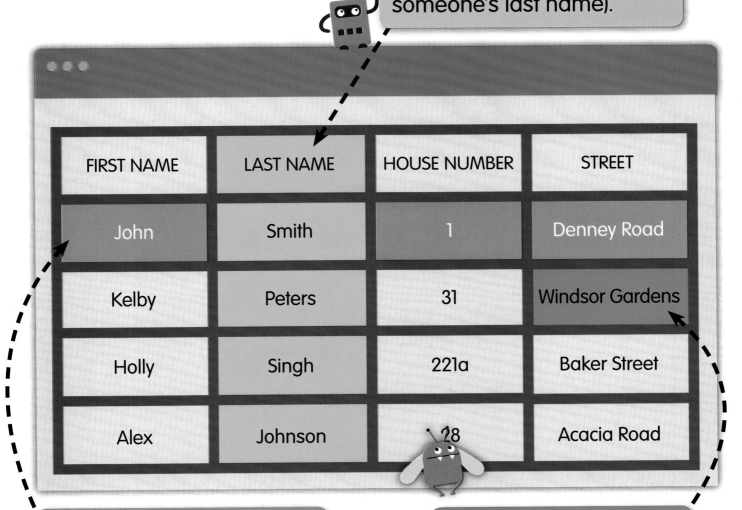

COLUMNS
Columns tell us the type of information (for example, someone's last name).

FIRST NAME	LAST NAME	HOUSE NUMBER	STREET
John	Smith	1	Denney Road
Kelby	Peters	31	Windsor Gardens
Holly	Singh	221a	Baker Street
Alex	Johnson	28	Acacia Road

ROWS
Rows hold the information – one for each record.

FIELDS
Fields hold the individual pieces of data.

WHAT CAN WE USE DATABASES FOR?

You can store any information like this in a database. A shop could store information about **customers** and orders, like this:

NAME	PHONE NUMBER	CAKE	PRICE
Kayleigh	202-555-0169	Large Chocolate Fudge Cake	$12.99
Emma	202-555-0130	Mississippi Mud Pie	$7.50
Elaine	202-555-0176	Fancy Lemon Cake	$14.00

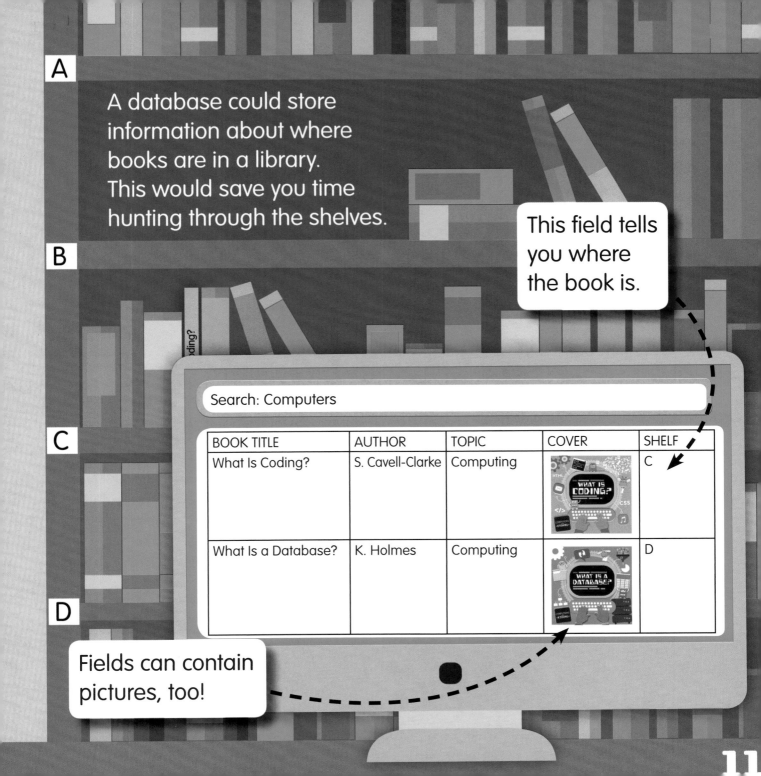

A database could store information about where books are in a library. This would save you time hunting through the shelves.

This field tells you where the book is.

Search: Computers

BOOK TITLE	AUTHOR	TOPIC	COVER	SHELF
What Is Coding?	S. Cavell-Clarke	Computing		C
What Is a Database?	K. Holmes	Computing		D

Fields can contain pictures, too!

11

WHAT CAN DATABASES DO?

Once your information is in the database, you can do things with it to make it more useful. You can add more information, look something up, or put the information in a different order.

FIRST NAME	LAST NAME	HOUSE NUMBER	STREET
John	Smith	1	Denney Road
Kelby	Peters	31	Windsor Gardens
Ho...	...ingh	221a	Baker Street
Alex	Johnson	28	Acacia Road
Garr...ett			

The data in this database is in a **random** order.

SORT IT!

You can tell a computer database to show your information in any order you want. You can sort a database using any of its columns. For example, you can sort all the first names **alphabetically**.

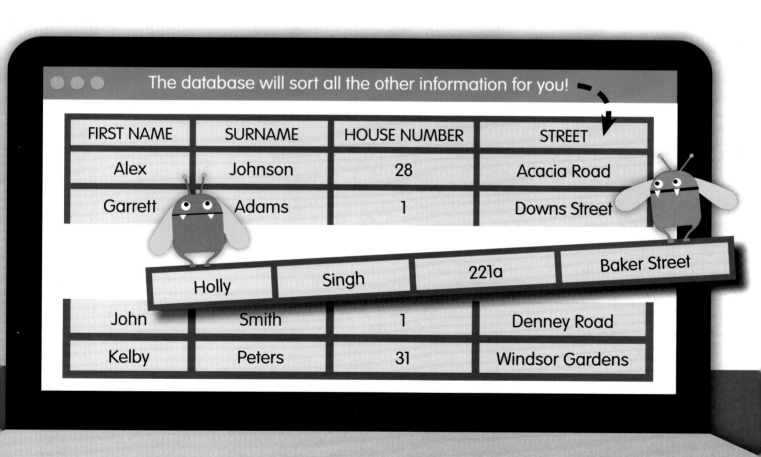

The database will sort all the other information for you!

FIRST NAME	SURNAME	HOUSE NUMBER	STREET
Alex	Johnson	28	Acacia Road
Garrett	Adams	1	Downs Street
Holly	Singh	221a	Baker Street
John	Smith	1	Denney Road
Kelby	Peters	31	Windsor Gardens

STORE IT!

Once you have entered and sorted your information, the computer can store it for you. You can choose to keep the information private, or you can share it so lots of people can use it.

SEARCH IT!

If you want to find information in a database, you can do a search to look up the information. The computer will look in all the fields and find it for you.

This saves you time, as you don't have to read the whole database to find the information you need!

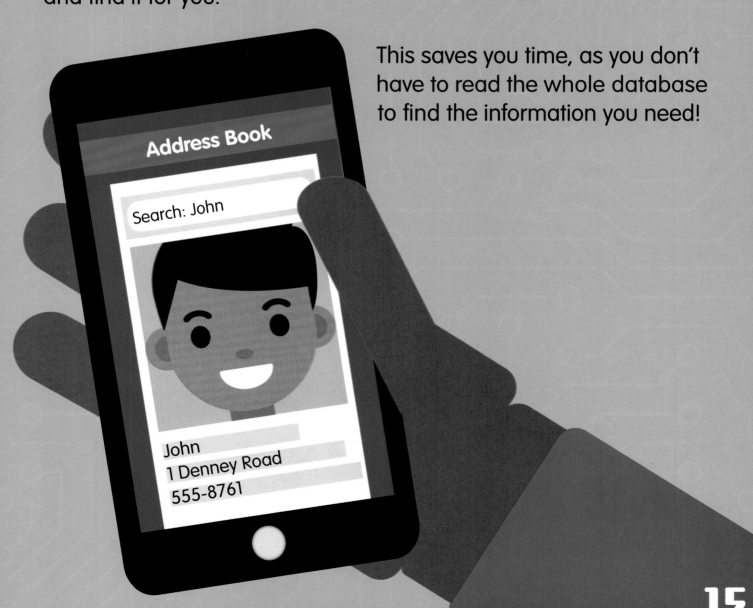

TYPES OF FIELDS

Databases have fields that hold different types of information.

TEXT fields contain only text: words, letters, numbers, and **symbols**.

	SURNAME	BIRTHDAY	AGE
Adams		March 30th	8
Drue	Hall	November 8th	8
Alex	Johnson	December 8th	7
Danielle	Martinez	May 21st	7
Kelby	Peters	January 3rd	7
Holly	Singh	September 14th	8
John	Smith	October 21st	8
Dan	Washington	February 21st	7

DATE fields contain calendar dates.

CALCULATED fields don't contain an entry – they work out sums or follow instructions instead.

GRAPHIC fields contain pictures. Graphic columns can't be sorted.

NEXT CLASS	ROOM	FAVORITE SUBJECT	PHOTO
09:00	15	Gym	
11:00	21	Computers	
09:00	15	Geography	
09:00	15	Art	
09:00	15	Music	
11:00	21	Science	
11:00	21	Math	
11:00	21	English	

NUMBER fields contain numbers. The computer can use these numbers in sums.

TIME fields contain clock times and can **automatically** update themselves.

DATABASES
AT HOME

We use databases at home and in our lives all the time. Let's see what databases we can find!

Social media sites store information about their users in huge databases.

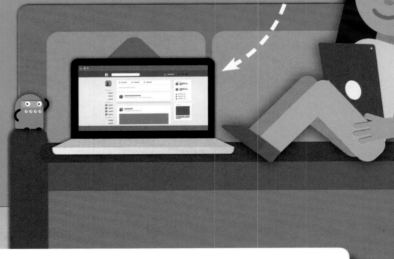

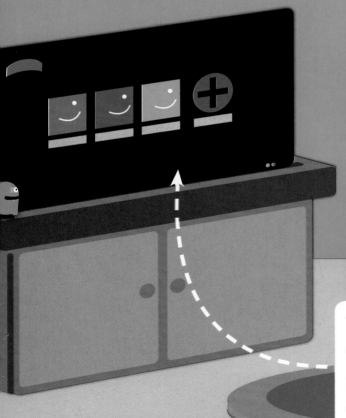

TV networks use databases to store TV shows, times, and information. You can search them for what you want to watch.

DATABASES
IN THE WORLD

Hospitals use a lot of databases. They store information about patients, including when they've been sick before, what medicines they have been given, and emergency contact details.

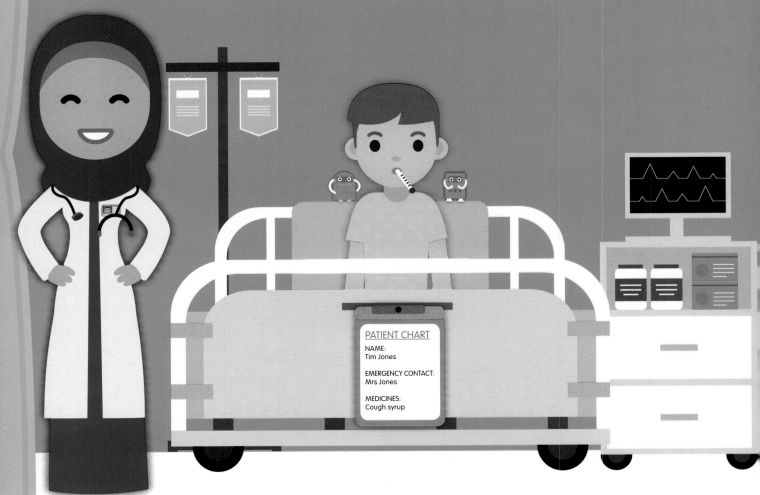

PATIENT CHART

NAME:
Tim Jones

EMERGENCY CONTACT:
Mrs Jones

MEDICINES:
Cough syrup

Supermarkets use databases to keep track of how many products they have. This helps the managers know when to order more.

BREAD $3

DID YOU KNOW?
When an item is sold and scanned, the computer subtracts that item from the database.

DATA PROTECTION

Once someone stores information, the law says they have to keep it safe. Personal information, such as names, addresses, and phone numbers, should be stored **securely** and not be shared.

TOP TIPS FOR
DATA SAFETY

Always protect any databases you have with a **password**. Make sure your password is hard to guess, but easy for you to remember. Use a mixture of letters, numbers, and special characters.

GLOSSARY

ACCESS	to get information
ALPHABETICALLY	in the same order as the letters of the alphabet
AUTOMATICALLY	without thought or control
CUSTOMERS	people who buy products or services
GPS	global positioning system; digital maps and directions
PASSWORD	a secret word or code used to gain entry somewhere
RANDOM	without a pattern or order
SECURELY	safely and without danger
SORT	put things in a particular order
SYMBOLS	images that represent something, such as a question mark
TOPIC	a subject or category

INDEX